Stakeholder engagement and strategies

Charith Venkat Pidikiti

February 2019

Author

Charith is a 1986 born, globetrotter and a biomedical engineer, who currently lives in Munich, Germany. A true jack-of-all-trades who religiously follows four words, "Ambition has no limits". Apart from being a full time employee at a Fortune 500 company, he is also an entrepreneur, an artist, a drummer, a fitness aficionado and a writer, who loves and collects classic cars and history books.

Hailing from India, a country rich in diverse religions and varied cultures, he was always obsessed with history, mythology and religion, yet it was his penchant for science since a young age that led him to study at the New York University, in one of the largest cosmopolitan cities of the world, NYC. After which he moved to work in Germany, where he is currently working on his Doctorate, has accomplished over four medical and two business publications and won the "Making A Difference" Award.

He constantly travels around the world with curiosity, learning foreign traditions, cultures, religions, modern technology or simply in pursuit of new experiences.

Follow the Author:

https://instagram.com/charithvenkat

https://www.facebook.com/charith.venkat

Copyright © Charith Venkat Pidikiti 2018

All rights reserved

Charith Venkat Pidikiti asserts the moral right to be identified as the author of this work.

Although the author and publisher have made every effort to ensure that the information in this book was correct at press time, the author and publisher do not assume and hereby disclaim any liability to any party for any loss, damage, or disruption caused by errors or omissions, whether such errors or omissions result from negligence, accident, or any other cause.

ISBN: 9781090582454

Cover concept and Design by Alpha-X

ANNOTATION

This book deals with the importance of stakeholder engagement for any organization and its business strategy, how to identify, plan and manage these stakeholders. The book also provides the recommended strategies one can employ to engage stakeholders (with overall benefits and risks), common issues faced and how to avoid or reduce these issues with the help of certain commendations, along with basic definitions of stakeholders together with the stakeholder theory. Both traditional approaches and emerging trends and new practices are outlines together with tools and techniques that businesses can employ which help in plotting stakeholders and structuring them in a visual and orderly fashion are described in this document. The book's main purpose is to provide different types of industries with knowledge on the importance of stakeholders and how they can make an informed decision to select a suitable strategy that is appropriate in their field and for their stakeholders. This book also provides readers with several examples from case studies regarding stakeholder engagement both about other companies around the world and the authors own experience and work environment.

KEY WORDS

Business

Company

Communication

Employee

Firm

Institution

Manager

Organization

Portfolio

Project

Staff

Stakeholder

Worker

TABLE OF CONTENTS

1. INTRODUCTION……………………………………….9
2. STAKEHOLDER…………………………………...…10
   - 2.1 Internal Stakeholders……………………12
   - 2.2 Connected Stakeholders………………..13
   - 2.2 external Stakeholders……………………15

3. STAKEHOLDER ENGAGEMENT……………..…..19
   - 3.1 Indentify stakeholders……………………22
   - 3.2 plan stakeholder engagement………….25
   - 3.3 manage stakeholders……………………27
   - 3.4 monitor stakeholders…………………….29

4. OTHER TOOLS AND TECHIQUES……………..32
5. CONCLUSIONS…………………………………...39
6. BIBLIOGRAPHY AND WEB RESOURCES…....43
7. TABLE OF FIGURES………………………………45
8. ABBREVIATIONS……………………………...46

INTRODUCTION

Any project, organization or process has several stakeholders involved who are either contributors or recipients of the results. Identifying these stake holders early on in the project or contract, planning these stakeholders' engagement and the communication with them, managing their needs and monitoring their engagement and influence are extremely important of the success of the project or the planned work that needs to be done.

All the aforementioned areas are in turn are very important for the organization and the managers to successfully engage the stakeholders which itself is important for the success of the organization and its endeavors.

Hence, stakeholder satisfaction is directly proportional to the success of the business and its outcomes, and to achieve this, the stakeholders need to be properly engaged which in turn is achieved when they are properly identified, classified, managed and engaged.

Several companies fail to succeed due to lack of knowledge on the subject of stakeholder engagement and the main goal of this book is it to explain the who, what and how of stakeholders and list the several strategies and tools one can use to assess the stakeholder engagement, with the main goal to help any organization or individual teams and departments to communicate, interact and involve each
identified stakeholder. These strategies are necessary for creating and sustaining positive relationships and involvement with stakeholders for successful business operations.

STAKEHOLDER

A stakeholder is either an organization, group or an individual who is impacted by the undertaking or result of any venture, program, portfolio or project within an organization and/or are effected by its activities, behaviors of its members, operations or goals. They may be affected in the short term or long term. They may be influential in the organization, oppose or support the decisions within the community in which it operates, hold relevant official positions or have an interest in the success of the undertaking, and can be outside or within the business that is supporting the project. Stakeholders can have a negative or positive effect on the project[1].

Several people are involved in bringing the project from start to a successful finish and it is very important to identify and manage each and everyone these stakeholders, including the ones that do not work directly under the management.

Stakeholders can be categorized broadly as follows:
- Internal stakeholders such as, managers and employees
- External stakeholders such as, environmental agencies and government
- Connected stakeholders such as, competitors, suppliers, shareholders or customers

---

[1]PMI – A Guide to the Project Management Body of Knowledge, sixth edition, September 6, 2017

Figure 1. Stakeholders influencing a business (Source: Strategic Management 2nd edition, Neil Ritson, Bookboon)

Internal stakeholders

These include but not limited to:

Managers: These stakeholders have a specific interest and apprehension for the growth and size if the organization or the business, its undertakings, status, job security, prestige (organization's' brand image, benefits from company, employees working under then, rank in position etc.), status quo and profitability.

Non-managerial staff: These stakeholders are usually have an interest in improvement in working conditions, salary, security of job, safety comparing to current situation of economy, industrial democracy and freedom from discrimination.

---

[2]Strategic Management 2nd edition, Neil Ritson, Bookboon

Employees: These stakeholders are highly productive when they are involved (or allowed participation) in decision-making, especially decisions that affect them. One major area for many companies as an organizational objective is Human resource development when they involve employees as a major stakeholder in decision making meeting etc. For example, Swedish company Volvo has developed a special job enrichment scheme for assembly line workers by introducing lean manufacturing, parallel flow, and dock assembly as supposed to semi parallel or serial flow. They have changed the way standard assembly line workers need to work[3]. Several German companies also have representatives from several working classes on the management boards called "Betriebsrat".

Connected stakeholders

These include but not limited to:

Customers: These stakeholders who are also the consumers and are primarily interested in advertisements, ethics, consumer protection and value for money. These stakeholders can be either government agency, hospital, institution, manufacturer, another company or even a distributor to a name few.

---

[3] Work at the Uddevalla Volvo Plant From the Perspective of the Demand-Control Model. Danielle Lottridge University of Toronto

Supplier: These stakeholders are interested in timely payments, a good deal or fair price, sustainable business and profits. Most companies acquire their services, equipment, raw materials or labor from external suppliers and uses them to produce an output. Advances in information processing and inventory control have made changes to the businesses' relationships with its suppliers. New concepts of having zero inventory called JIT or just in time are saving many companies huge sums of money from having storage spaces or warehouses and the cost of owning or leasing those properties which come with maintenance and personnel. This results in more suppliers, supply chains, and a network of close relationships between these suppliers and the organizations consisting of quality control and lead-time deliveries.

Competitors: These stakeholders are interested in the degree of competition between each other in their own industry and the range of the potential threat or rivalry from the entry of new players into their industry or territories. Competitors are the challenging forces against the business, its underlying economics and exist in any industry and in several forms.

Shareholders: These stakeholders supply any additional risk capital and are owners of firms or investors in the company, depending on the requirement. There are generally two types of shareholders that any company has and these types will mostly define the type of information that can be acquired from them. These two types are institutions (generally large size) or private shareholders (small group of investors or individuals). Examples include pension funds, insurance companies, institutional investor, investment trust companies, unit trusts etc.

External stakeholders

These include but not limited to:

Governments: These stakeholders are interested to seek finance via taxes or other means, gaining political support, gaining votes through legislated activities, safety, and harmony within the industry or within industries, privatization aiming at increasing competition and efficiency.

Pressure groups: These stakeholders are interested in the quality of life, pollution reduction, poverty eradication, green peace, fair trade, sustainability, global welfare, ecosystem preservation, and reduction of wastage, disturbance of nature or ecological balance and prevention of use of non-renewable resources.

Often times all the different types of stakeholders are involved (in large manufacturing firms) and are closely linked to each other as depicted in figure 2. In other words, the pressure groups could force the government to make a new regulation that will cause changes to a company's product, this will cause the shareholders to invest more money to mitigate this risk and in turn cause a change in the suppliers' orders and the employee might need new training. Finally, the customers receives a product that had to be changed a certain way to comply to the regulation.

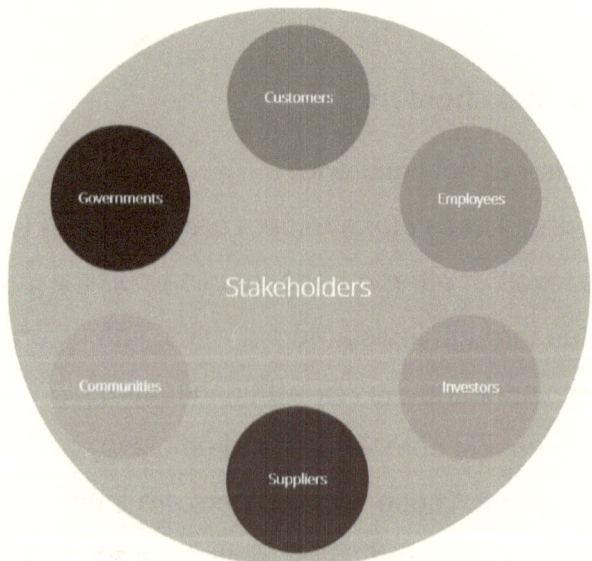

Figure 2. Internal, connected and external stakeholders (Source: https://corporatefinanceinstitute.com)

One such example is the inclusion of catalytic converts to Ford cars to reduce harmful exhaust fumes and in turn minimize pollution, which in turn increased the cost of the car irrespective of whether or not the customer wanted this part. The inclusion of the catalytic convertor might have been due to pressure groups protesting which in turn caused the government to reach and issue a new regulation. The exhaust system supplier needs to modify the exhaust system or create the catalytic convertor and the employee needs to engineer and fit the part. The cost of the catalytic convertor is transferred to the consumer. The U.S. Environmental Protection Agency's regulation of exhaust emissions requires that, catalytic converters must be fitted to of vehicles since 1975[4].

Another example is the company Intuitive Surgical that makes robots for performing minimally invasive surgeries. These robots such as the daVinci Si, daVinci Xi and Ion each serve a specific purpose and have to go through stringent phases of regulations, animal and clinical trials. Each one of these systems also have a 6-month preventive maintenance service cycle that is mandatory to ensure safe operation of the systems. The daVinci robot was first developed by NASA and DARPA to create a remotely controllable surgical robot that can be setup either in the International space station or in a war zone so that the surgeon can operate remotely from a safe location. Over the years the number of stakeholders

(Internal, connected and external) have gone up bringing the surgical systems to mainstream markets where surgeries are performed on a regular basis due to its several advantages which include, faster post-operative patient recovery times, ease of use, minimally invasiveness, and reduction surgeon fatigue to name a few. Naturally, the regulations for such a new product have been constantly evolving, as no such product has existed before for the governing bodies to use from historic repositories. Surgeons are discovering new ways and new procedures to use the surgical robots (started with simple thoracic procedure and now any procedure is possible). This has attracted more biomedical engineers (connected), patients (customers), hospitals and their management (external) and OR staff (internal) as well to join the list of stakeholder.

---

[4]Air Pollution, the Automobile, and Public Health.Watson AY, Bates RR, Kennedy D, editors. Washington (DC): National Academies Press (US); 1988.

STAKEHOLDER ENGAGEMENT

A process by which an organization involves individuals or groups who may, positively or negatively influence the decisions, be impacted by the decisions made or executed by the undertakings of the organization is known as stakeholder engagement. Stakeholder engagement is the most important subject of any organizations' CSR or corporate social responsibility is stakeholder engagement that involves achieving the three bottom lines otherwise known as TBL, which includes social (people), environmental/ecological (planet) and financial (profit) frameworks[5].

I order to improve the accountability and decision-making; companies identify and engage their stakeholders who in turn help the company identify which environmental and social matters are most important to them in terms of their performance.

Stakeholder engagement is also a requirement for certain certification, standards organizations, auditing and governing bodies such as the Global Reporting Initiative (GRI) and International Organization for Standardization (ISO). Stakeholder engagement is essential for any kind of

---

[5]Slaper, Timothy F. and Hall, Tanya J. (2011). "The Triple Bottom Line: What Is It and How Does It Work?" Indiana Business Review. Spring 2011, Volume 86, No. 1.

governmental and non-governmental organizations (NGOs), labor organizations, businesses, financial institutions, industry and trade organizations.

The main advantage of stakeholder engagement is they have an opportunity to be a part of the decision making process of both public and private sector organizations, which can have long-term effects and solutions for complex issues or issues of concern. In other words, it gives the organization an ability to influence and interact with the stakeholders for the overall benefit of their ventures and its sponsors.

Academic research shows that catastrophes that have occurred during any undertaking inadvertently traced back to poor management of stakeholders, which highlights the importance of a structured method to identify, prioritize and engage all the involved stakeholders.

There are 7 core principles for the achievement of successful engagement of stakeholders[6]:
- Plan stakeholder engagement; collect and incorporate key stakeholders' feedback(iterative process together with stakeholder identification) and communicate with

---

[6]Jeffery, Neil (2009). "Stakeholder Engagement: A Road Map to Meaningful Engagement". The Doughty Centre for Corporate Responsibility, Cranfield School of Management. Retrieved 23 April 2015.

stakeholders regarding implementation of feedback or measure taken/not taken and reasons for it.
- Understand or identify the stakeholders
- Management and alignment of the stakeholders, Conflict resolution e.g. through meetings.
- Building trust with the stakeholders
- Consulting with the stakeholders
- Respond and implement corrective or preventive actions
- Monitor evaluate and document stakeholder engagement

The difference between a business' success and failure depends on the management and the team to properly identify and engage the stakeholders in orderly fashion. It is for this reason that stakeholder engagement should commence immediately after they have been identified.

Identify Stakeholders

The first step after understanding who a stakeholder is will be to identify all the stakeholders who have an interest and can or will be impacted by the organizations efforts. Identifying stakeholders is the process of evaluating and recording all relevant information regarding the stakeholders, their, influence, interdependencies, involvement, impact and interests on the project success. This process enable the organization to identify the right strategies for engaging each individual stakeholder or a group and is the key to the management's success.

Examples of these people can include but are not limited to the following:

- Consultants to the project
- Group impacted by the project after its completion
- Group impacted by the project as it progresses
- Line managers
- Product testers
- Project customer
- Project user group
- Project leader

- Project team members

- Resource managers

- Senior management

- Subcontractors to the project

One good tool for identifying stakeholders and their relationships is a salience model, which can place the stakeholders into categories such as power, legitimacy and urgency.

Figure 3 is an example of one such salience model showing areas, which can help, identify and place the stakeholders depending on their power, legitimacy and urgency and further into dormancy, danger, dependency etc. This model provides managers with the ability to plot stakeholders within three dimensions. There are three main categories used; power, legitimacy and urgency (described previously). Stakeholders can fall under either category or even several or all categories; hence, managers can plot the stakeholders in 7 categories as see in figure 3.

Definitive stakeholders represent all (power, urgency and legitimacy) followed by Dominant, Dependent or Dangerous stakeholders representing two of the three attributes.
For this purpose, a Venn diagram is used as shown below.

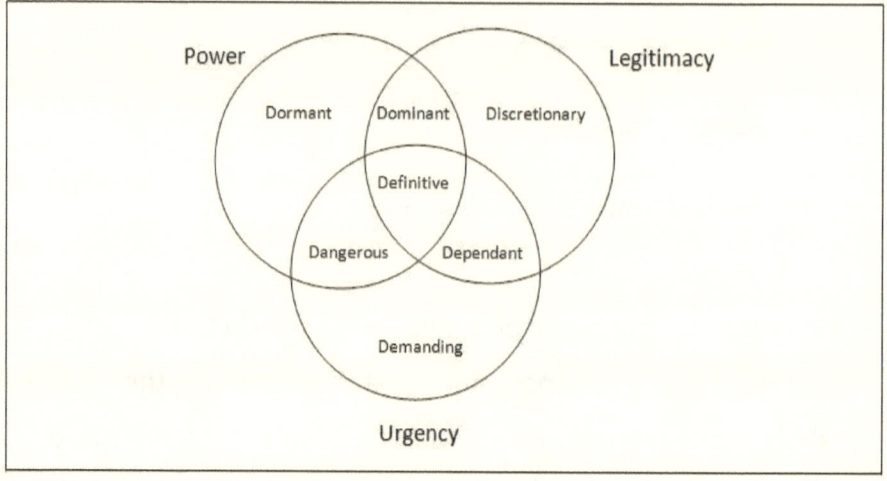

Figure 3. Salience model showing the areas. (Source: www.velopi.com)

The categories mentioned could each be ranked in order of their prominence to identify the amount of attention needed for each type of stakeholder.

Plan Stakeholder Engagement

In this process approaches to involve the identified stakeholders into the work done by the organization as part of the strategy is developed. The involvement is typically done based on the stakeholders' potential impact, interests, expectations and needs on the project. This process provided the plan to effectively interact with the stakeholders and is performed periodically[7]. It is a good strategy to develop an initial plan (first version) for stakeholder engagement as soon as the initial stakeholder group is identified.

A good practice would be to start with mind mapping to visually consolidate the stakeholders' information and their connection within the organization and with each other. One this is done, all the data can then be entered into a stakeholder engagement assessment matrix. The data can then be further categorized to identify their level of engagement as following:

- Unaware – The state where the stakeholders are unaware of the project or its impacts.
- Resistant – The state where the stakeholders are resistant to changes to the planned work.

---

[7]Waitemata DHB Stakeholder Engagement: Strategic Plan

- Neutral – The state where the stakeholders are neither supportive not resistant.
- Supportive – The state where the stakeholders are supportive of the organization's work.
- Leading – The state where the stakeholders are actively engaged in making sure the organization's work is a success.

Figure 4 shows an example of engagement levels of three stakeholders where "C" represents current state and "D" is the desired state. The management and team set the desired level of engagement of each stakeholder and using this stakeholder engagement assessment matrix the organization can use their strategies to bring the individual stakeholders to the position they consider best for their planned work.

Stakeholder	Unaware	Resistant	Neutral	Supportive	Leading
Sponsor				C	D
Dept. managers	C			D	
Contractor		C		D	
Employees				C D	

Figure 4. An example of stakeholder engagement assessment matrix (Source: www.researchgate.net)

Manage Stakeholder Engagement

This process involves working and communication with the stakeholders with the intention to meet their expectations, needs, redress their grievances and foster their involvement appropriately in the work performed. This not only allows the management to increase their support levels but also minimize the stakeholders' resistance to the business endeavors.
A good strategy would be to prioritize the stakeholders (since there will be several) in terms of their relative importance to this business. For example, one stakeholder might play a pivotal role in acquiring permissions while another might be only responsible for giving legal advices.

Recommended successful stakeholder's engagement strategies are:
- Involving the stakeholders in the design and implementation of the stakeholder engagement process, right from the start of the project.
- Active listening, to understand the stakeholders' interests and concerns which in turn helps the business interest.
- Addressing concerns related to risks and threats towards managing stakeholders
- Resolving and clarifying identified issues
- Anticipating issues raised by stakeholders in the future

- Ensuring the expectations of the stakeholder are met through communication and negotiation
- Acquiring sustained stakeholder commitment at several phases of the organizations on-going work by engaging them consistently
- Good communication skills, together with open communication policy.
- Collection of feedback from stakeholders through meetings and surveys
- Good interpersonal and team skills such as, conflict management and political/cultural awareness

Following the above-mentioned points are recommended for ensuring a positive relationship with the stakeholders and that all the objective are met, for the business' success.

Monitor Stakeholder Engagement

This process involves monitoring the relationships of the stakeholders and tailoring different strategies to engage them. The primary benefit of monitoring stakeholder engagement is that it ensure that the effectiveness and efficiency of the stakeholder engagement activities is maintained or even enhanced as the environment of the organization or its projects evolve. It is a good practice to always check in with the stakeholders to see how things are going once a stakeholder engagement plan is in place. The manager should always ask himself, is there anything that can be done to improve communications or is there something that can be done to enhance the stakeholders' involvement. In monitor stakeholder engagement, one should always check to see if the plan to engage the stakeholders is being followed[8].

---

[8]Redefining Stakeholder Engagement: From Control to Collaboration Pamela Sloan The Journal of Corporate Citizenship No. 36 (Winter 2009), pp. 25-40

Figure 5 is one of the recommended tool to use here is multicriteria decision analysis, where all the criteria for engaging stakeholder successfully are weighted and prioritized, which in turn help in identifying the most suitable choice. Another tool that is also useful is a stakeholder engagement assessment matrix, which helps in tracking changes in the stakeholder engagement levels for each stakeholder. This will help the organization increase its efficiency of stakeholder engagement as the project evolves. Its is also very important to review the lessons learned register from business archives, issue logs, organizational risk register as defined the communication management plan of the business.

Not only is it important to monitor the stakeholders it is also important to evaluate them, such as carrying out performance evaluations, e.g. did the vendors deliver on time? Was funding provided when needed in a timely fashion?

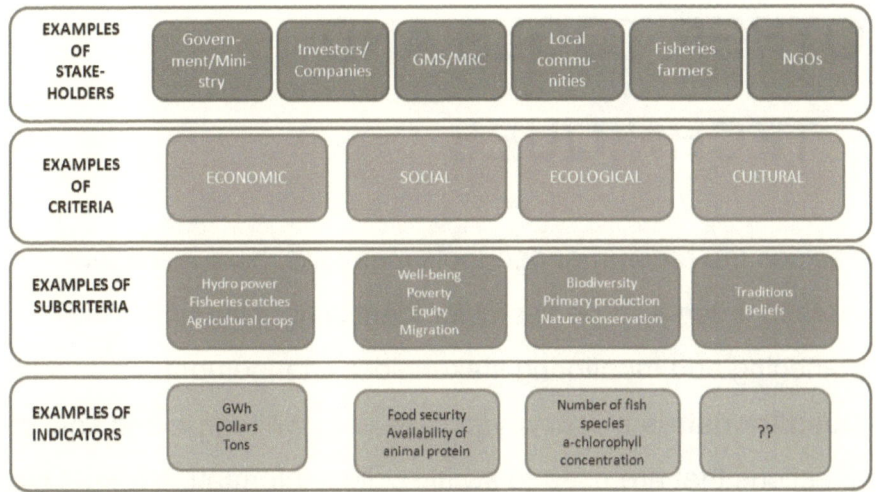

Figure 5. A hypothetical scheme of potential stakeholders, criteria, sub criteria and indicators related to hydropower development projects. (Source: http://environment.sal.aalto.fi/MCDA/)

The difference between a business' success and failure depends on the management and the team to properly identify and engage the stakeholders in orderly fashion. It is for this reason that stakeholder engagement should commence immediately after they have been identified.

OTHER TOOLS AND TECHNIQUES

Besides the recommended tools mentions, here are a few more that can also be useful for identifying, planning, managing and monitoring stakeholder engagement:

Questionnaires or surveys: These are written/printed sets of questions that are used to swiftly collect information from a big group of people. Questionnaires and surveys are the most suitable method of collecting feedback when the audience/stakeholders are highly varied, or the stakeholders are highly dispersed globally, when a statistical analysis is desired or when a quick response (turnaround) is required.

Brainstorming: This is a tool used to quickly identify, gather and develop a list of stakeholders who could be potentially involved in the business. Ideally, a facilitator in a group environment conducts this technique and it comprises two parts, firstly ideas are generated as a list and secondly they are analyzed. Brainstorming can also be used to collect data and ideas from the stakeholders or collect solutions to a problem from team members or subject matter experts. E.g., IBM's program „Innovation jam" is known to encourage their employees to brainstorm for bringing new ideas to their products.

Brain writing: This technique provides individual stakeholder or teams with certain amount of time to consider each one of the questions before the facilitator begins the session. This can be said to be a modification to brainstorming. The data is generally collected in either direct fact to face sessions or virtually such as mobile apps, web browsers, video conferences or emails E.g., Think tanks of Earth Institute, New York are known to be one of the most influential groups that use brainstorming[9].

Stakeholder analysis: This technique helps create a stakeholder list with all the relevant data like their positions within the company, roles in the organization, their stakes, attitudes, needs and expectations, support levels and interests.

These stakes are as follows:
- Interest of a group or individual who is affected by a decision made by the organization.
- Rights, which are either legal rights such as, safety, occupational health (defined in the legislation of the respective countries) or moral rights such as, sustainability, environmental, ecological or historical sites' preservation and protection.

---

[9] Aronsohn, Marie „Lamont Climatologist Testifies on Capitol Hill About Sea Level Rise", 27 February, 2019, http://earth.columbia.edu/

- Ownership of an individual or group of stakeholders having the legal title of ownership to a property or an asset.
- Knowledge which is either general or specialist, an individual stakeholder has can be of prime benefit for the organization. An organization can take advantage of this knowledge towards an effective executing on its deliverables, objectives, and outcomes.
- Contribution from stakeholders in the form of funds or other resources such as, human resources, or support in the form of advocacy, legal advices, forming a buffer between the power structures in an organization, the projects and the politics that surround or simply promoting the objective of the organization.

Power/influence, power/interest or impact/interest grid:
These techniques helps in grouping the stakeholders based on their power or authority level, interest or concern levels on the organizations decisions, influence or the capacity to impact the outcomes of the organizational decisions, the ability to make changes to execution or planning in the organization. These models for classification are highly beneficial for stakeholder communities or small-scale industries with simple relationships between the business structures and its stakeholders.

Figure 6 shows an example of a power/interest grid that allows for placing stakeholders based on their authority level and concern levels

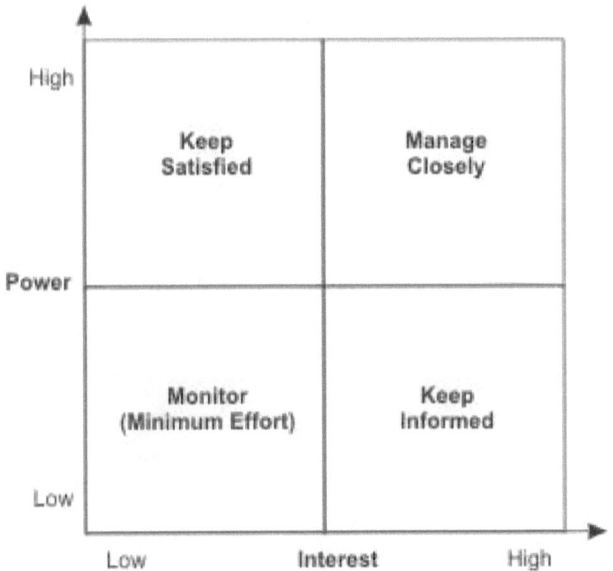

Figure 6. Power/interest grid (Source: https://www.researchgate.net)

Stakeholder cube: This technique give a three-dimensional approach to the Power/influence, power/interest or impact/interest grid models that combines all the elements into one cube that can be very beneficial to the organization in engaging the stakeholders and to identify them. This model enhances the representation of the community as an entity that is multidimensional and helps in the development of business strategies and communication.

Figure 7 is an example of one such stakeholder cube that shows several dimensions and elements as a single model. Power is plotted on the Y-axis, competence or influence along the Z-axis and interest along the X-axis. The list of stakeholders are then plotted within the cube.

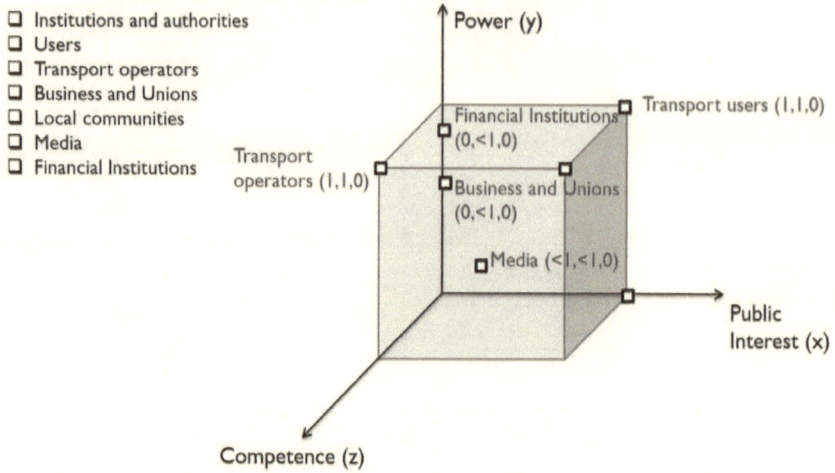

Figure 7. Stakeholder cube showing power, interest and competence along its axis (Source: www.researchgate.net)

Directions of influence: This technique categorizes stakeholders according to their relative impact/influence on the business or the organization and are categorized as follows:
Upwards such as senior management within the company, steering committee, board of directors or customer organization/sponsor.
Downward such as the performing organizations team, specialist or technical engineers etc.

Outward such as suppliers, end-users, government organizations or regulatory bodies.

Sideward such as management peers, product managers, collaborators, other managers sharing common resources etc.

Prioritization: This technique is important in making a ranking system when there are there are large number of stakeholder when the stakeholder community is very complex or when they are constantly changing.

Root cause analysis: This technique aims at identifying the causes for an issue with the stakeholder community, what the reasons for each individual complaint is or what the reason for not meeting their needs and expectations are etc.

Assumptions and constraint analysis: This techniques helps in collection assumptions from different teams on who the stakeholders potentially could be and where the stand/what their stake are.

Mind mapping: A visual method to quickly place stakeholders based on their relationships to each other and the business.

Feedback/presentation: Collection of feedback and giving presentations are a simple yet effective ways to gather information from all stakeholder and communicate effectively which then regarding distribution of information.

Voting: this is a critical factor in helping to select the best response for a variance in stakeholder engament.

Meetings: this technique helps in gathering information regarding stakeholders from a large group either face to face or virtually.

These tools help to visually map the stakeholders in a structured manner, allowing for ranking, positioning and updating which are very important to know the current status of the respective company's stakeholders.

CONCLUSIONS

Stakeholders are the most important for any business to succeed. Constant usage of results to review strategies and techniques for stakeholder engagement throughout the lifecycle of a business, in order to increase project support and maximize improvements to stakeholder engagement. The key to effective engagement is continuous communication the each one of the stakeholders and the team members. This enables the management to involve all the stakeholders in business activities and decisions, manage any interest conflicts and issues which occur and finally to understand and meet the expectations and needs of them. Managers can provide the internal stakeholders with mediums to engage with communities/ connected stakeholders and other external stakeholder via online forums, discussion boards, and digital knowledge base (library). These mediums offer tools like resources and social performance guidance where participants can discuss, seek advice or ask questions. Internal, connected and external can exchange information with each other and even post continuous updates, which provides guidance and best practices. Management can use this information to develop meetings or working groups to focus on integrating the solutions into their business planning and processes within the organization.

Strong stakeholder engagement involves tracking the effect of all the business initiatives, and its impact on the communities in which the business operates, while maximizing accountability and transparency. Stakeholder satisfaction should be one of the main business objective and should be identified and managed early in the formation.

Recommendation: It is a good practice to develop an initial plan (first version) for stakeholder engagement as soon as the initial stakeholder group is identified. These identified stakeholders should then be prioritized based on their influence and interest and then implement the most appropriate communication methods and select the right content to communicate, next involve the stakeholders in the organization and its project as much as possible, collect feedback and check if their needs are being met. Management should ensure that the stakeholders get the necessary information after their feedbacks have been considered and/or implemented. This is performed through an optimal communication channel and will ensure that the stakeholders get up to date information on risk, opportunities and key performance indicators of business operations. Manage the stakeholders by use of appropriate training, meeting expectations, company notifications, and consistent reporting. Use of specific resource management soft wares can be helpful in collecting the data from the stakeholders and organizing that information which also aids in rapid input, tracking and cross-referencing all that information. Next is stakeholder information reporting and good reporting will maximize transparency and accountability and minimize risk or threats to the company and its processes. The last and most important step is Stakeholder Relationship Analysis and Improvement; all the collected data and feedback from stakeholders should be analyzed and used as lessons learned to continuously improve current stakeholder engagement and strategies or develop new strategies for future.

The key benefits with proper stakeholder engagement are:
- Offers prospects to refine the alignment of business practices with the social needs
- Helps in driving long-term sustainability of the organization
- Increases the shareholder values
- Helps in competing in the constantly changing and increasingly complex business environment
- Development of market
- Improved risk management
- Innovation of new strategies, processes and products
- Enables systemic change towards development of the organization

Key risks of not engaging stakeholders are:
- Ambiguity of result

- Digression and diversion of resources
- Divisions and factions within all the levels, Silo thinking
- Emotional Incompetence
- Possibility of reactive planning
- Unethical or unprofessional behavior

Effective identification, understanding and management of your stakeholders, their expectations and their triggers will improve the company's ability to minimize risk, develop mitigation measures and deliver a successful outcome.

BIBLIOGRAPHY AND WEB RESOURCES

- Watson AY, Bates RR, Kennedy D, "Air Pollution, the Automobile, and Public Health". Washington (DC): National Academies Press (US). 1988.
- Ezekiel Chinyio, Paul Olomolaiye, John Wiley & Sons, "Construction Stakeholder Management". 22 Oct 2009
- Corporate finance institute, "Stakeholder", https://corporatefinanceinstitute.com/resources/knowledge/finance/stakeholder/
- Aronsohn, Marie „Lamont Climatologist Testifies on Capitol Hill About Sea Level Rise", 27 February, 2019, http://earth.columbia.edu/
- PMI, "A Guide to the Project Management Body of Knowledge", sixth edition, Project Management Institute – September 6, 2017
- Pamela Sloan "Redefining Stakeholder Engagement: From Control to Collaboration", The Journal of Corporate Citizenship No. 36 (Winter 2009), pp. 25-40
- Sequeira, Debra et al. "Stakeholder Engagement: A Good Practice Handbook for Companies Doing Business in Emerging Markets". 2007. International Finance Corporation

- Jeffery, Neil (2009). "Stakeholder Engagement: A Road Map to Meaningful Engagement". Cranfield School of Management, The Doughty Centre for Corporate Responsibility, Retrieved 23 April 2015.
- Neil Ritson, "Strategic Management 2nd edition", Bookboon
- Slaper, Timothy F. and Hall, Tanya J. "The Triple Bottom Line: What Is It and How Does It Work?" Indiana Business Review. Spring 2011, Volume 86, No. 1.
- Waitemata DHB Stakeholder Engagement: Strategic Plan

TABLE OF FIGURES

Figure 1	Stakeholders influencing a business	Strategic Management 2nd edition, Neil Ritson, Bookboon
Figure 2	Internal, connected and external stakeholders	https://corporatefinanceinstitute.com
Figure 3	Salience model showing the areas	http://www.velopi.com
Figure 4	An example of stakeholder engagement assessment matrix	https://www.researchgate.net
Figure 5	A hypothetical scheme of potential stakeholders, criteria, sub criteria and indicators related to hydropower development projects	http://environment.sal.aalto.fi/MCDA/
Figure 6	Power/interest grid	https://www.researchgate.net
Figure 7	Stakeholder cube showing power, interest and competence along its axis	https://www.researchgate.net

ABBREVIATIONS

ADS	American Depositary Share
CSR	Corporate social responsibility
GRI	Global Reporting Initiative
ISO	International Organization for Standardization
JIT	Just in time
NGO	Non-governmental organization
TBL	Triple bottom lines

www.ingramcontent.com/pod-product-compliance
Lightning Source LLC
Chambersburg PA
CBHW021936170526
45157CB00005B/2330